ANGER

SHANNON B. RAINEY

Dr. Tom Varney
Series Editor

BRINGING TRUTH TO LIFE
NavPress Publishing Group
P.O. Box 35001, Colorado Springs, Colorado 80935

The Navigators is an international Christian organization. Jesus Christ gave His followers the Great Commission to go and make disciples (Matthew 28:19). The aim of The Navigators is to help fulfill that commission by multiplying laborers for Christ in every nation.

NavPress is the publishing ministry of The Navigators. NavPress publications are tools to help Christians grow. Although publications alone cannot make disciples or change lives, they can help believers learn biblical discipleship, and apply what they learn to their lives and ministries.

Cover illustration: David Watts

All Scripture in this publication is from the *Holy Bible: New International Version* (NIV). Copyright © 1973, 1978, 1984, International Bible Society. Used by permission of Zondervan Bible Publishers.

Printed in the United States of America

4 5 6 7 8 9 10 11 12 13 14 15 / 99 98 97 96 95

CONTENTS

FOREWORD

ह&

Someone has said that the root of all sin is the suspicion that God isn't good. If that thought is correct, then the presence of sin should never be surprising. What we witness in life is evidence that does not make it easy to believe that God is as good as He claims.

Tragedy touches all our lives. Buried memories, too painful to face, continue to haunt us with their unrecognized power. Our really good relationships (and they are few) seem indelibly stained with flaws that keep us quietly discouraged with an ache that cannot be fully dulled. Good times come, but they reliably go. We get a promotion, and then a kidney stone. We feel good when we check off the items on our "to-do" list, then the car won't start. And in the face of all that He allows, God refuses to apologize; He never withdraws His invitation to us to taste and see that He is very, very good.

To people who live somewhere on the continuum between the opposite endpoints of unusual blessing and extraordinary suffering, the invitation to taste God's goodness may seem a mockery. Those on either end may see it differently. With facile ease, they proclaim God's goodness in the midst of plenty; and with desperate hope, they cling to His goodness when there is nothing else. But most of us spend most of life in the middle—with not quite enough blessings, and with difficulties that usually seem survivable.

This provides us with the luxury of looking closely at our lives—and complaining. When life's circumstances or some internal experience nudge us along the continuum toward the endpoint of tragedy, our complaints intensify. Our sense of justice is offended: "On top of everything else, now this! It just isn't fair." We feel righteously enraged.

Our anger seethes, sometimes turning into loud explosions of violence, other times remaining in check but obvious. While it is always present with a power that harms and destroys. Beneath our efforts to continue living, we clench our fist at God and scream, "You are not worthy of trust!"

That is how most people live their lives, mapping out a strategy for moving along from the starting point of a clenched fist toward an untrustworthy God. Like Cain, who thought God's requirement that he wander was unfair, we set out to build a city for ourselves where we can find happiness and rest whether God cooperates or not.

But it never works. Our cities always have problems. Except for those temporary times when everything seems to be working as it should and those other times when things are so bad that hope in God's goodness is all that's left, we stumble along trying to cope with the range of irritations life presents. Misplaced car keys, social snubs, pregnant daughters, more money owed than made, discouragement that replaces joy, lifeless sermons, attractive but off-limit secretaries: not an hour goes by when something doesn't trigger our anger.

Rather than merely working to control our anger, perhaps there is a place for exploring it (as we take responsibility for controlling its sinful expression). It is my understanding that anger reveals a fundamental problem within us that requires serious and long-term attention.

In this study, Shannon Rainey peeks in through the window of anger to a room that is normally shut off to visitors, and often even to oneself. She turns on the light and makes the mess visible—the mess behind the anger that needs to be cleaned up. Her intention is not to scold us for our wrong patterns of displaying anger, but to expose a worse problem that will direct us toward deeper trust in God as good—and with that trust, toward an unclenched fist.

All of us struggle with anger. It's part of being alive in an imperfect world with the legacy of Adam: an attitude that questions God's goodness and, therefore, takes over responsibility for the impossible task of making life work. Let this booklet guide you into a biblical way of thinking that can replace the consuming passion of anger with the burning joy of love.

DR. LARRY CRABB

INTRODUCTION

୨ଈ

We all get angry. Even God gets angry. Unfortunately, our anger is rarely as loving and constructive as God's. Some of us do tremendous damage to other people through our anger, while many prefer to do tremendous damage to ourselves. Either way, we find it hard simply to decide one day to handle our anger differently. The Bible says, "In your anger do not sin" (Ephesians 4:26), but understanding how to manage that will require a close look at ourselves and the Bible.

This guide is intended to help you take that close look. It can be used in any one of three ways: (1) on your own; (2) with a group after prior preparation at home; or (3) with a group with no prior preparation.

It's amazing how another person's story can spark insights into our own situation. A discussion group shouldn't get larger than twelve people, and four to eight is ideal. If your group is larger than eight, one way to be sure everyone gets plenty of time to talk is to divide into subgroups of four to discuss. This approach can accommodate even a large Sunday school class.

You'll get the most out of the guide if you use both prior preparation and group discussion. Group members can read the text of a session and reflect on the questions during the week. They might keep a journal handy to jot down thoughts, feelings, and questions to bring to the group time. This approach allows time for participants to recall and reflect on incidents in their lives.

However, a group can also approach the sessions "cold" by reading the text aloud and answering the questions together. If busy schedules make homework impractical, feel free to take this approach.

Finally, if you're using this guide on your own, you'll probably want to record your responses in a journal.

The guide is designed to be covered in six sessions of sixty to ninety minutes each. However, you could spend a lot more time on some questions. If you have plenty of time, you might want to travel through the guide at your group's own speed.

Each session contains the following sections:

A warm-up question. You'll be coming to sessions with your mind full of the events of the day. To help you start thinking about the topic at hand, the sessions begin with a warm-up question. It often refers to what you've observed about the anger in your life during the previous week. At other times, it invites participants to let the others get to know them better.

Text. You'll find words of insight into the topic in each session. Sometimes the text appears in one chunk; at other times questions fall between blocks of text. You'll probably want someone (or several people) to read this text aloud while the other group members follow along. Alternatively, you could take a few minutes for each participant to read it silently. If you've all read the text before your group meets, you can skip reading it again.

Discussion questions. These will help you understand what you've read and consider how it relates to your own experience and struggles. Each participant's stories will shed light on what the others are going through.

When the text is broken into two or more sections,

with questions in between, you should discuss the questions before going to the next section of text.

Many questions ask participants to talk about themselves. Everyone should feel free to answer at his or her own level of comfort. People will often feel some discomfort if a group is really dealing honestly with the issues. However, participants should not feel pressured to talk more personally than they wish. As you get to know each other better, you'll be able to talk more freely.

Prayer. Ideas for closing prayer are offered as suggestions. You may already have a format for praying in your group, or you may prefer not to pray as a group. Feel free to ignore or adapt these ideas.

During the week. In this section, you'll find ideas for trying what you've learned and for observing your daily behavior more closely. Feel free to do something else that seems more helpful.

Process notes. The boxed instructions will help the leader keep the group running smoothly. There are also leader's notes at the back of this guide.

Whether you're a group leader or a participant, or using this guide on your own, you'll find it helpful to read the introduction to this series from the Institute of Biblical Counseling: *Who We Are and How We Relate* by Dr. Larry Crabb. It explains the reasoning behind this series' approach to handling problems.

6.
16.
8.
8.
8.
6.
14.
_____
66

WHAT IS ANGER?

❧

LEADER: Open the session by explaining what the group should expect in this and the next five group sessions. You'll be examining the common human experience of anger through biblical eyeglasses. In this session, you'll begin by identifying what that experience is like for each of you.

You may want to open the meeting with prayer. Then ask each person to introduce himself or herself (unless participants already know each other) and answer question 1. Write down the questions participants raise.

---

1. What is at least one question about anger that you would like God to answer? Can you think of more than one?

LEADER: Ask one or more people to read the following material aloud. While they read and listen, ask participants to underline statements they identify with.

ME? ANGRY?

A few years ago a friend asked me if I ever got angry. I told him I couldn't think of the last time, or really *any* time, that I was truly angry. Oh, sure, sometimes I felt frustrated, maybe a bit irritated, and certainly inconvenienced, but I assured him that I simply was not an angry person.

But he knew my life. He knew that when I was a child I used to run away from home. Perhaps I had been justly rebuked for disobeying my parents or starting a fight with my sisters. Sometimes I ran away to escape the outbursts of anger I couldn't help overhearing from my parents, who were separating. Other times I felt ignored and unsupervised and thought I would see how long I could be gone before my disappearance was noticed. (On those occasions I climbed the large magnolia tree in our front yard and waited, usually until I had to scramble down to use the bathroom.) I even remember running away because I didn't like the food I was forced to eat. (Brussels sprouts, yuck!)

In all these situations, I had not gotten my way. Try as I might, I could not make my world work the way my young but stubborn will had determined things should go. Instead of directly acknowledging and/or expressing my anger or hurt, I simply left the scene altogether.

As I grew older, running away was not socially acceptable when one was upset. So I learned to hide my emotions and "disappear within myself," while remaining physically present. A warm smile and interest in others worked well to mask what was going on inside me. When asked if I was angry about some situation, I'd brush it off as no big deal. My friends had a hard time believing I wasn't angry when my boyfriend of three years broke up with me, but my response was to blame myself and thus avoid any feelings of anger toward him.

My denial worked well enough to convince myself

14

and others that I could rise above such negative emotions. Me? Angry? Never!

DISCOVERING MY ANGER

My marriage, however, blew away some of my false illusions. Perhaps for the first time in my life, I could no longer fool myself about my anger. I couldn't escape those feelings of rage that always come as two selfish sinners live in such close proximity to one another. But I still thought I could hide my anger from my husband.

For instance, when we returned home from our honeymoon, we couldn't find $200 we'd received as wedding gifts. David declared that *he* certainly did not misplace the money, so it was obviously my fault. I was not about to claim absolute innocence in the matter, but neither was I prepared to take 100 percent of the blame. I thought in marriage all things, whether good or bad, were shared. For richer or poorer, right? We turned our neat little apartment upside down looking for the cash, but to no avail. I was boiling inside for having been blamed. Whatever happened to innocent until proven guilty? But I'd be darned if I was going to let my new groom see my anger. Instead I quietly withdrew and nursed my wounds in privacy.

Two months later, when I was flipping through my coupon file in a kitchen drawer, I found the $200 and faced the moral dilemma of whether to tell David or just spend the cash and keep my mouth shut. I took him out to a nice restaurant and revealed the lost and found treasure. We laughed and almost cried about something that had just about provoked my desire to leave my husband — in keeping with my strategy to withdraw rather than face my anger.

Whether we want to admit it or not, anger is a universal emotion that all of us experience. We differ in the extent of our awareness of anger and in how effectively we deal with it, but the fact is that none of us can escape anger.

15

HOW WE CHOOSE A STRATEGY

As common as anger is, though, many of us have been taught that anger is bad or sinful, so we deny our own angry feelings and avoid others who are angry. Some form their attitudes toward anger directly from their parents, either mimicking them or choosing the opposite behavior. I concluded at an early age that anything was preferable to the expressions of anger I witnessed from my parents. My mode of survival was denial. Others learn to deal with anger according to the standards of church or Sunday school, and grow up wearing their "smiley faces" and fearing condemnation for negative or angry feelings.

While many deny their anger, others have learned that anger can be exploited for getting one's own way. Some children grow up in an environment where power is wielded through selfishness, cynicism, hatred, and violence. Such attributes may be rewarded in the offspring as well. Rewards may come subtly when a child's temper tantrum wears down the parent and gets the child what he wants. Some families hand down anger through racial prejudices or by affirming a child for beating up the neighborhood bully. In such cases, children learn that uncontrolled outbursts of fury are not only acceptable, but also effective in forging their way through life.

Whether we deny or exploit our experiences with anger, there is no doubt that anger is a powerful emotion, a mighty passion that can be constructive or destructive. If we harness our anger and set a godly course for its expression, anger can move us to act with integrity and love for the sake of others. Also, if we face our angry responses to life's disappointments, anger can expose our own desperate need for a sovereign, loving God.

So anger can be powerfully channeled for the good and protection of others and mightily used to deepen our own need for the gospel. But more often, the power of our anger harnesses us and wreaks havoc in our souls and destroys relationships. Therefore, many people fear and avoid anger — their own and others'. Yet unaddressed anger does not just go away; it lodges in our character, infects our approach to life, and may fester into more intense and pervasive forms, including deep bitterness, subtle hatred, and violent rage.

Anger offers a window into the soul — a glimpse into one's longings, pain, and style of relating to others. Isn't it wise, then, in the context of a safe and caring community, to learn more about ourselves by examining and exposing the anger that some of us wear on our sleeves and others go to great lengths to mask?

THE DYNAMICS OF ANGER

While anger is not necessarily positive or negative, it *becomes* good or bad, righteous or sinful, constructive or destructive, based on its dynamics: its symptoms, sources, and functions; and our ways of dealing with anger.

In this guide, we will look at each of these dynamics. First, we'll ask, "What does anger look like?" We'll see many faces or masks of anger, many *symptoms* of behavior and individual styles that express or repress this emotion. Once we have identified anger's various guises, we can recognize our own symptoms and styles of anger.

We must also examine anger's *sources* and consider, "Where does anger come from?" Often our anger is rooted in selfishness and sin; at times it may be rooted in righteousness. What's the difference?

Perhaps the most telling dynamic of anger is its *functions* or purposes. The question "What does anger do for us?" cuts to the core of the issue and probes the motives of our hearts.

Next, our sinful distorted styles of dealing with this emotion will be discussed and finally contrasted to the only true way to experience *healing* from anger: through the power of the gospel, which compels us to love and forgive others as we have been loved and forgiven by God.

These dynamics of anger coalesce to give anger its moral value. For while anger is not innately positive or negative, it ultimately takes on a definite moral character. All anger works either *for* or *against* others, ourselves, and ultimately God.

2. What have you learned to believe about anger in the course of your life? (Select as many as apply.)

   ❑ Anger is almost always negative in my experience.

   ❑ Anger should be avoided if at all possible.

   ❑ Anger should be dealt with head on.

   ❑ Anger is a great way to get what I want.

   ❑ Understanding what I'm angry about lets me know what I'm really after in a situation.

   ❑ There's no point in getting mad. It won't make any difference.

   Other ideas?

3. *(Optional)* If someone you know were to answer question 2 about you based on your behavior, what would he or she say? (If you're really brave and know each other well, ask someone in the group to tell you how he or she would answer question 2 for you.)

4. a. How did your parents handle their own anger?

b. How did they handle others' anger?

5. What did you learn from your parents' example?

6. How do you usually feel when someone expresses anger to you?

   ❑ I stiffen and become defensive.

   ❑ I go numb and try to sidestep the issue.

   ❑ I am easily provoked to anger in return.

   ❑ I feel sick to my stomach.

   ❑ I feel ashamed and want to either confess guilt or hide.

   Other feelings?

7. a. Look up Matthew 5:21-24. Jesus is talking about the standards of life in God's Kingdom. Why do you think Jesus views anger as equivalent to murder? (Why is it so serious?)

   b. How easy is it for you to live up to this standard? How do you feel about that?

8. Read John 2:13-17. Most people agree that Jesus is very angry in this passage. Why do you suppose He thinks anger is okay in this situation?

9. What would you like to change about the way you deal with anger?

LEADER: You've spent most of this session determining your starting points: what you each already think about anger and perhaps where you got those ideas. (When you're pursuing change, it's always nice to know where you're starting from.)

In session 2 you'll again be looking at the present: What's your unique way of expressing (or repressing) anger? From there, you'll begin looking beneath the surface to see why you do what you do and how you can shift to a more constructive style.

STILLNESS

To close this session, you could try a simple format for prayer. First, during a few moments of silence, participants can collect their thoughts. Then each person should have a chance to tell or ask God something. For instance:

- God, right now I'm feeling _____, and what I'd really like to know is_____.

- Thanks, Lord, for _____.

If praying aloud is new for your group members, you may want to start with praying just one sentence each.

DURING THE WEEK

As you go through the next few days, try to be aware of when you are angry. Pay attention not just to overt anger, but also to signs of subtle anger, such as withdrawing. Try to observe *what* you get angry about and *how* you show anger. You might want to jot notes to yourself as it happens or at the end of the day.

SESSION TWO

THE SYMPTOMS OF ANGER:
What Does Anger Look Like?

୬୶

1. Briefly describe a time when you were angry during the past week. If you don't remember feeling angry, do you recall feeling frustrated or depressed?

> LEADER: Give each person a minute or two to answer question 1 before you move to the text. Ask one or more people to read this material aloud. Ask participants to consider, as they listen and read along, whether they tend to repress their anger or express it.

Anger can have an uncanny variety of appearances. Some wear it well-disguised, while others flash their anger like a neon sign. But there are two basic styles in which we all dress our anger. We either *repress* and stuff this emotion, pretending it isn't there, or we *express* and dump our anger like dirty laundry for all our neighbors to see.

23

REPRESSION

The thought behind the repression of anger goes like this: "My angry feelings are awful. Therefore I will hide them beneath an acceptable (pleasant, virtuous, pious) mask and hope that they will soon disappear." In many families and churches, people are commanded — either specifically or by implication — not to feel problem emotions such as anger, fear, or jealousy. This instruction produces pretense, personal problems, shallow relationships, and lost opportunities for growth. The problem with this advice not to feel troublesome emotions is that, to a remarkable extent, humans are capable of just that.

One woman I counseled was married to a man who had a history of affairs, both before and during their marriage. Lindsey knew about her husband's unfaithfulness, but instead of confronting him and letting him see her hurt and anger, she would reaffirm him, telling him what a great father and provider he was.

During one session, Lindsey recognized her fear of abandonment, which began almost as early as the day she was born. Her natural parents had given her up for adoption, and before she was finally placed with her adoptive parents, she lived with four foster families. Several years later, her adoptive parents divorced, and once again she faced the prospect of being unwanted and passed on to someone else.

The pain of feeling unwanted and abandoned was so excruciating for Lindsey that she stuffed her heartaches as well as her legitimate anger beneath a mask through which she praised her husband. But she was deeply resentful. Lindsey's fear of being left all alone, her pain over her husband's repeated unfaithfulness, and her "need" to trust an untrustworthy man, generated a bitterness that she had denied for over ten years.

But her denial of her anger was self-protective. To admit her fears and anger to herself, much less to her husband, might lead to a confrontation in which Lindsey would risk losing her husband and ending up where she was at birth: unwanted and alone. Refusing to take this risk, she adeptly concealed her anger from herself and others, and survived with a resulting chronic, low-grade depression.

The point is that our hearts are capable of hiding strong emotions, particularly anger and rage, but we cannot escape the damage wrought by repression.

In addition to depression, there are many other guises or symptoms of repressed anger. Stuffing one's anger may look like naive denial with a sickeningly sweet facade (like Lindsey), or withdrawal and avoidance of others (as was my chosen style), or even self-destructive and compulsive behaviors — overeating, abuse of drugs and alcohol, and sexual promiscuity. All of these masks are attempts to cover up one's anger from oneself and others, and to hide or make up for the effects of anger by substituting other symptoms.

EXPRESSION

This belief is behind expressing anger: "My anger is a legitimate part of me, and I will therefore express it if and when I want to." There's less need to describe what dumping or expressing anger looks like because we've all seen it in its many faces. Expressed anger may appear as sarcasm; verbal outbursts; aggressive, malicious, and hostile behavior toward oneself or others; violence; and even murder.

Often, as people mature and begin to face rather than deny the disappointments in their lives, they acknowledge deep-seated feelings of anger. A client I'll call Randy was working with me to deal with his abusive past. The more conscious he became of the torturous events in his life, the stronger the emotions he experienced and the angrier he got.

After each counseling session Randy would inevitably explode at someone. One week he yelled at his boss and was let go. Another week he threw objects around his apartment, breaking glass and lamps, and shortly thereafter his roommate moved out. You can imagine the effects on his relationship with his girl-friend, who for unhealthy reasons did not leave him. In all areas of his life, Randy had lost control and allowed his anger to take over.

When he spent an entire counseling hour lashing out at me after there was no one left to abuse, I said, "Randy, no amount of angry outbursts will take away the pain you feel inside, just as no extent of past vic-timization justifies the damage you are doing to others. Are you willing to face and talk about what's truly bothering you in the next session?"

Randy's indiscriminate expressions of anger had accomplished no good for himself and certainly were not in the best interests of others. Though his mask of expressed anger was more overt than Lindsey's subtle and disguised repression, it did not serve him well in dealing with his painful past.

TARGETS OF ANGER

Whether we repress or express our anger, it is directed toward one of two main targets: self or others.

Repressed anger taken out on ourselves may lead to such self-sabotaging symptoms as procrastination or compulsive overeating. Though these symptoms look different, they both are ways of taking our focus off the original anger, punishing ourselves with the consequences of missed deadlines or excess weight, and then providing reason to be mad at no one but ourselves. Repressed anger that is subtly directed toward others may be a condescending, devil-may-care, or I-don't-need-you attitude. These are never addressed head on, but can be perceived by others nonetheless.

On the other hand, expressed anger taken out on ourselves may include self-abusive talk ("I'm such a fool" or "I can't do anything right") or more violent gestures — cutting oneself or even suicide. Expressed anger aimed at others may show itself through gossip, cursing, beating, or murder.

The two basic styles of anger, repression (or stuffing) and expression (or dumping) interact with two main targets, ourselves and others, to create many faces of anger — some of which go undetected and certainly undealt with. That's why we need to undress this emotion in its various subtle and disguised *symptoms* before we can get to the *sources* that arouse our anger.

2. Do you tend more often to repress or express your anger? Specifically, how do you do that? (Choose as many as apply.)

Repress
❑ Feeling depressed

❑ Pretending niceness while burning inside

❑ Withdrawing

❑ Condescending to others

❑ Procrastinating

❑ Overeating

Other ways of repressing:

Express
❑ Rebuking yourself

❑ Hurting yourself physically

❑ Gossiping

❑ Yelling at others

❑ Hitting others

❑ Breaking dishes or other objects

Other ways of expressing:

3. Why do you suppose that's your chosen style?

4. Are you surprised that any of the above (such as depression) are symptoms of anger? Explain.

5. Who is most often the target of your anger? Why do you think you have chosen that person(s)?

6. *(Optional)* Psalm 31:9-13 depicts depression and how it insidiously permeates every level of our being.

   a. How does the psalmist describe his depression? Can you identify with his feelings?

   b. How does he work through the experience with God in prayer in the rest of the psalm?

   c. In verses 17-18, the psalmist begins to express his anger to God in rather blunt terms. How would it feel for you to say this kind of thing about the people you are angry at?

d. Do you think the psalmist was wrong to express this kind of anger in his prayers? Why do you think that?

STILLNESS

Each participant should take a minute or two to read through Psalm 31 and choose *one verse* that suggests something you'd like to say to God in prayer. Take turns reading your chosen verse aloud and praying a sentence or two about it.

Example for verse 4: *Father, I feel trapped by _____, and I have no one to rely on but You. Please free me, and help me to trust You to do that.*

DURING THE WEEK

As you did last time, watch for situations in which you become angry. Observe times when you express your anger and also for when you repress it, such as through eating, withdrawal, or depression. Jot some simple notes like these:

Express or Repress	How?	At Whom?	Why?
E	Shouted	Son	Didn't do chores
R	Stayed late at work	Wife	Felt belittled
E	Cursed	Self	Lost keys

If you didn't take time as a group, you may want to look at Psalm 31 on your own. Would you pray verses 17-18 about your enemies? Why, or why not?

THE SOURCES OF ANGER:
Where Does Anger Come From?

è&

1. If you brought them, look over your notes on angry situations during the past week. Share with the group one or two of the situations in which you found yourself responding with anger. You can also share anything else you found interesting (maybe you expressed anger toward yourself more often than you realized).

> LEADER: Give everyone a chance to answer question 1. Then read the following material aloud. Have group members ask themselves, "What is the source of my anger?"

DESIRES

What do the following angry people have in common: a little girl who was sent to her room, a teenager who was rejected for a date, a secretary who was mistreated by an inconsiderate boss, and a parent whose child has a terminal illness? Some may feel that life is unfair; others that life just shouldn't be so hard. But

31

every one of them feels hurt; none of them has gotten his or her own way.

At first glance, it looks like the anger experienced by all of these people comes from external circumstances, often beyond their control. In each case, something happened *to* them. Presumably, feelings of anger would not have been aroused if the opposite occurred: for instance, a little girl is praised for good behavior, a teenager is asked to the prom, a secretary is given a promotion, and a parent has a healthy child.

It's easy to claim that the source of our anger lies in someone or something outside ourselves, to argue that other people's actions against us warrant our angry responses. But more often than not, external factors are invalid excuses for our anger.

In contrast to our typical focus on *external* causes, the Bible points to *internal* sources of anger and bitterness. In James 4:1-3 we read,

> What causes fights and quarrels among you? Don't they come from your desires that battle within you? You want something but don't get it. You kill and covet, but you cannot have what you want. You quarrel and fight. You do not have, because you do not ask God. When you ask, you do not receive, because you ask with wrong motives, that you may spend what you get on your pleasures.

We often feel angry when we don't get what we want. But our anger comes not so much from the external circumstances as primarily from the *desires* that rage within us. The angrier we feel, the more strongly we believe internally that the thing we didn't get externally is what we need and must have to live.

SELFISHNESS

If our unmet desires are the cause of much anger and infighting, what are we supposed to do—not want? *No!*

James tells us that we are to ask God for our desires. The problem is, we ask with wrong motives. Our motives are tainted through and through with self-seeking goals instead of a desire to love and serve others. The force behind most of our anger really is the stubborn sin of selfishness!

Another source of anger (hardly worth mentioning because it is the exception rather than the rule) is holy anger against sin. Purely righteous anger is reserved for the Lord. We have much to learn from this rare source of anger, which will be studied in the last session.

Without stereotyping all singles groups, I'll use an illustration, from my past before I married, of my experience among fellow unmarried friends. Most of us women were interested in being treated as special by the single men in our fellowship. The "desires that battled within us" for love and enjoyment of relationships were natural and God-given. After all, there was nothing wrong with wanting to be chosen. But what we often did with our desires was utterly selfish.

When we couldn't rejoice with an engaged friend, when we bickered in meetings to have the upper hand in planning social events, and when we griped about how wimpy the men were because they didn't ask us out, our desires were anything but warmly inviting. Instead, we were consumed with self-centered energy that ignited anger and jealousy, distanced the men, and alienated the women into competitive factions.

When we tired of the "fights and quarrels among us," we'd go through stages of denying our desires, hiding our jealousy, and disguising our anger behind an exasperated facade of thinking, *Men! Who needs them anyway?!*

Ultimately the motives underlying our desires were self-seeking. When we did not get our way, we wore our anger in its various guises, with no real concern for how we could encourage our brothers or rejoice with our sisters who were dating frequently.

33

BLOCKED GOALS

When we want something and don't get it, our goals are blocked. Rather than feel the pain and disappointment of a blocked goal, we tend to react with anger. Anger seems to hurt less and even helps to numb the pain, so it is often our automatic response.

Think back to Randy's story in the last session. As a child he longed for his parents' love and protection, yet received their hatred and abuse. As an adult, when he was on the verge of facing how badly he had been damaged, he believed he would be absolutely destroyed by the pain he felt, the shame he had suppressed, and the emptiness that consumed him. Instead of facing these feelings and his disappointment, Randy got angry at everyone he could. He felt more in control when he was acting out his anger (although he was actually out of control), than when he was thinking through his uncontrollable past. Anger was Randy's chosen response because it hurt less, and thus he felt perfectly justified in his violent reactions.

Want something + don't get it = blocked goal → anger

LEADER: Let one person respond to questions 2 through 4, then let another person respond — rather than going back and forth between people. In this way, you'll focus on one person's situation at a time. Keep an eye on the clock to make sure that everyone gets a chance to discuss a situation. If your group is large, divide into subgroups of three or four for this section.

---

2. Think of a recent time when you felt anger (or its disguises: depression, withdrawal, a self-destructive compulsion). What blocked goal was at the root of your anger?

3. In what ways was this goal selfish or loving? Explain.

4. Are you aware of any hurt or sadness that your anger, like Randy's, might be covering? Explain.

LEADER: Ask someone to read the next section aloud.

SELF-JUSTIFICATION

While anger is most often rooted in our self-centeredness, it is forcefully propelled by our self-justification. When we're angry, we're blinded to our own faults as we focus on the injustices committed by others. In the midst of anger, our selfish responses seem so reasonable to us. We feel that any mature person, perhaps even the Lord Himself, would share our indignation. This self-justification works in our hearts, seemingly excusing us from any responsibility to care for others, while we are busy taking care of ourselves.

Lindsey's husband, Cliff, was caught up in this cycle of self-centered anger fueled by self-justification. When he married Lindsey, he expected all his needs to be fulfilled in this one relationship and that his struggle with promiscuity would disappear. But instead of being an exciting spouse, Lindsey was a fearful and needy person herself.

In the first months of their marriage, whenever Lindsey would cry, Cliff would leave the house. He was ticked off that she apparently wanted more from him than he had to give. So Cliff would go to other female friends for consolation. When they offered him relationships with no demands, he felt perfectly justified in

35

having affairs. He rationalized that, after all, the affairs never lasted very long (how could they, with such a selfish orientation?), he always returned to Lindsey, and she somehow seemed happier afterward.

Cliff told me that as long as he didn't hurt anyone (he was deceiving himself that he wasn't hurting Lindsey, his lovers, or himself), any means justified getting what he thought he wanted: his way with no hassles. Still, it was one thing to be upset that his marriage was not as satisfying as he had hoped, but quite another to demand angrily that his needs be met and to justify whatever action seemed necessary to meet them.

When we set about to justify our anger, we find that its roots are not merely in our raging desires, but in our *demandingness* to have these desires met in our own way, in our own timing. This demandingness to have what we want when we want is ultimately rebellion against God — an arrogance that feigns more wisdom and control than the Creator of the universe has.

ANGER ULTIMATELY AGAINST GOD

Most of us won't readily admit our subtle anger toward God, even hatred of Him. But all too often, we find the requirements of God's law of love too exacting, and we resent Him for putting us in what feels like an impossible situation. When we can't blame anyone else for our troubles, God becomes the culprit.

Jack is a hardworking man who was laid off from his job in the lagging economy. He has pounded the pavement and his church members have prayed about employment for him for over a year, yet still no prospects. Has God deserted him? Doesn't the Lord care about his family's situation? To "consider it pure joy" when he faces "trials of many kinds" (James 1:2) seems ludicrous to Jack, while anger at God seems reasonable. But anger at God is not mentionable in his church, so Jack's anger goes underground and emerges in the form of a lack of energy for spiritual matters, distancing himself from the Lord and His people.

In short, the common source of anger has more to do with internal selfishness than with external circumstances. When our desires become *demands* that feel totally justified to us, our resulting anger is ultimately arrogant and defiant rebellion against God—whether subtle or overt.

Legitimate desire → *self-justified demand* → *anger against God*

5. Think about the blocked goal you described in question 2. What signs of demanding your way or justifying yourself do you see in your response?

6. What signs of anger against God do you see in your responses to current situations? Think about how you would complete the following sentences. Then summarize your thoughts with the final sentence.

    ■ I'm mad at God because He won't give me . . . .

    ■ I'm mad at God because He won't give me . . . soon enough.

    ■ I'm mad at God because He insists that I . . . and I don't want/feel able to do it.

    I'm mad at God because . . . .

STILLNESS

To close, you can pray together about anger toward God. Here are some options.

- Confess your anger.

- Ask God to show you anger you're unaware of.

- Thank God for reaching out to you even while you're so rebellious.

- Ask God to help you let go of your anger toward Him.

DURING THE WEEK

Watch for blocked goals and demands this week. When you find yourself frustrated, upset, or depressed, ask yourself these questions:

- What is my goal?

- Am I demanding my way?

- How am I rebelling against God?

THE FUNCTIONS OF ANGER:
What Does Anger Do for Me?

ﻉﺀ

1. Describe a situation in which you were angry during the past week. What was your blocked goal? What did you want that you didn't get?

LEADER: Give everyone a chance to answer question 1.

We get angry when our goal is blocked. But anger does more for us than just allow us to let off steam. As you read the following material aloud, ask participants to listen for the three functions of anger and think about how those apply to the angry situations they just described.

Most people would say they don't like their own or other people's anger. It's not pleasant to be around, it feels unpredictable and uncontrollable, and it often damages those in its path. Why, then, do we hold on to our anger like a security blanket? Why do we not really hate but instead love our anger? Anger must work for us to accomplish some conscious or preconscious goals. Anger has three major functions.

PROTECTION

Anger is a protective shield. We can use it to cover
the painful places in ourselves, as is most common;
or we can arouse our anger to cover others and their
painful places. Remember Lindsey, who submerged
her anger toward her unfaithful husband in order to
soothe or hide the intense pain she would have felt
had she dealt honestly with her life? Her long-term
anger disguised through depression and numbness
"worked" for Lindsey to sinfully protect herself from
lifelong hurts. Her anger functioned to cover her own
wounds.

Contrast that picture to the one we see of Jesus in
Matthew 16:21-23:

> From that time on, Jesus began to explain to
> his disciples that he must go to Jerusalem and
> suffer many things at the hands of the elders,
> chief priests and teachers of the law, and that
> he must be killed and on the third day be raised
> to life.
>
> Peter took him aside and began to rebuke
> him. "Never, Lord!" he said. "This shall never
> happen to you!"
>
> Jesus turned and said to Peter, "Get behind
> me, Satan! You are a stumbling block to me; you
> do not have in mind the things of God, but the
> things of men."

When Peter protested against Jesus' upcoming
death, the Lord responded with powerful, but controlled anger. The anger Jesus felt in response to Peter's
ignorant protest was not for His own protection, but for
the protection and welfare of others whose eternal life
depended on His brutal death and glorious resurrec-
tion. Rarely do we use our anger in a legitimate way to
sacrificially protect those we love, for we are too busy
using our anger illegitimately to take care of our own
wounds.

40

REDIRECTION

Anger can serve not only to protect, but also to redirect the energy and passions stirring within us. When we are hurt and react in anger, we can manage both to defend ourselves and to attack the opposition. Anger becomes an indispensable weapon: It first gets the focus off our own pain, then inflicts it elsewhere.

Anger also moves the spotlight away from our own sin, so it is a masterful tool for shifting blame. For example, a wife had been stashing her husband's money in a secret place. When he found it after snooping around, she was so enraged that she managed to redirect the focus from her sin of the original deception and breach of trust in hiding the money to his sin of violating her privacy. Her anger also avoided the real issue behind stashing the money: She lived with debilitating fear and insecurity concerning both her material and emotional needs, trusted no one to provide for her, and resorted to her own devious schemes to offer her an illusion of security.

Anger can also divert and re-channel the passions within our soul. Melanie was a victim of severe sexual abuse throughout her childhood. As she was working through these issues and was beginning to remember and put words to what had happened to her, she would feel overwhelming urges to cut herself and pull out her hair in fury. The internal scars were too excruciating to face; she preferred to take her rage out on herself and shift the focus to her bloody wrists and thinning hair, which were incomparably less traumatic to her than her hemorrhaging soul. Melanie's anger and self-inflicted wounds provided temporary relief to her by numbing her deepest anguish and shame.

Many of us resort to more subtle ways than Melanie's of shifting the focus away from our deepest hurts to other secondary problems. We might angrily overspend rather than face issues of a dysfunctional family. Compulsive overspending creates new and more obvious problems (debt and creditors at the door) and avoids the more painful family issues where the real anger and underlying hurt reside.

DISTANCING

A third function of anger is that of putting others at a distance. Instead of being open to relationships, we use our anger to snuff out our tenderness, to spit in the face of our longings for intimacy, and to push people away.

Although hardness of heart and isolation from others is *not* what we want most deeply, at times we choose such distancing anger in order to avoid the risk of being disappointed and getting hurt again. We feel more in control when we push people away than when we remain open to relationships and either move toward others or vulnerably invite and wait for them to pursue us.

Both dumping and stuffing anger can successfully keep people out, either by stabbing them or by building a wall around ourselves. A rebellious adolescent who has never been loved enough to be disciplined is hostile and crass with everyone he meets and has no friends, yet craves more than anything the involvement and strength of someone who would care enough to handle him. The rage he wears on his sleeve communicates to the world, "To hell with you, leave me alone," while internally his heart is whimpering, "Please come after me!" The angrier he acts and the more daring his illegal activities, the more successful he is at silencing his heart's cry for love.

WHY HOLD ON TO ANGER?

These three functions of anger—protection, redirection, and distancing—work well enough that we continue to rely on their services. But the truth is that anger works at cross purposes to what we were built for—namely, dependence on God and enjoyment of relationships. If we are truly trusting God to protect us and to enable us to deal with whatever we face in life, then we can resign

42

from our self-appointed job of protecting ourselves and redirecting the focus away from our sins and scars through the use of anger.

Furthermore, if we are striving to love the Lord our God with all our heart, soul, mind, and strength and to love our neighbor as ourselves (Mark 12:30-31), we will not seek to employ our anger to distance ourselves from relationships.

2. Think about the angry situation you described a few minutes ago, or something you've been angry about for a long time. How did your anger accomplish some of these functions? (It may not have fulfilled every one.)

   a. To soothe or hide your pain.

   b. To redirect your passion from your own pain to inflicting pain on someone else.

   c. To shift the spotlight from your sin to someone else's.

   d. To push people away.

   e. To snuff out your tenderness and longing for intimacy.

3. What do you think is wrong or sinful about each of these functions of anger?

4. How do you suppose the functions of righteous anger would be different? You can look at the example of Jesus in Matthew 16:21-23 or of Moses in Exodus 32:19-29.

STILLNESS

To close, talk with God about the ways you use anger. Everyone should have a chance to confess wrong ways in which they've used anger. Ask God to make you aware of your wrong motives for anger during the coming week. Is there anything you want to thank God for?

DURING THE WEEK

As you catch yourself getting angry this week, take a minute to explore how your anger serves to protect you, redirect attention, and/or distance you from people.

STYLES OF DEALING WITH ANGER

1. When you were angry at some point this week, what is one thing you did to handle it?

   ❑ Gritted my teeth.

   ❑ Recited Scripture to myself.

   ❑ Blew up.

   ❑ Told a joke.

   ❑ Examined the goals of my anger.

   Another way you handled anger:

LEADER: While reading this material aloud, participants should think about which approach to anger sounds most like them.

The symptoms by which we express or repress our anger are linked to our views about the best ways to deal with anger. We'll look at three ineffective styles

of managing anger and contrast these with the way of
using anger for the sake of love.

THE STEEL MAGNOLIA

One style seems typical of Southern women like
myself who have been trained to be "Steel Magnolias."
Expected to be beautiful and composed, and somehow to handle the pain of life with smiling faces, Steel
Magnolias must be strong, repress their anger, and handle it—whatever "it" may be.

In the movie *Steel Magnolias,* the character Clairee
denied her hurt and repressed her anger by minimizing
any offense and handling life through laughter. Truvy,
the beauty parlor operator, repressed her rage and
agony by living vicariously through other people's stories to avoid her own, and covering unattractive feelings
with makeup.

Shelby, perhaps the greatest denier of reality,
believed there was no time for worry. She got pregnant and tried to be as strong as she could, until her
one transplanted kidney failed her. Her philosophy of
"you just grit your teeth and do what you have to" led
to her premature death. M'Lynn, the petite matriarch
of the town, expressed it best when she said, "It's the
men who are supposed to be made of steel, but it's the
women who are counted on to be strong, to be present
at the beginning of life and at the end of death." She
was so mad she didn't know what to do, except, of
course, to be strong and handle it.

This submersion of anger and rising above it all
certainly has its counterparts in men as well as women,
not only in the South but everywhere. The underlying
assumption of this approach is that direct anger is
not allowed, not acceptable, not helpful, not ladylike,
and/or not worth it. Anger is repressed behind a steel
front of strength and pretense.

One positive outcome of this approach is external
damage control: for the most part, others don't get hurt.
But neither do they get helped, because they receive

neither tenderness nor even clear feedback about how they affect us. Steel Magnolias can neither speak the truth in love nor offer their passion and compassion.

The real danger of this approach, however, is the toll it takes on the person's soul. Steel Magnolias may not openly run over others, but they inwardly drive themselves to the grave. Repression ultimately results in self-destruction.

THE NICE CHRISTIAN

A second style of handling anger leads not to self-destruction but to self-condemnation. Instead of repressing it altogether, this approach dismisses anger by quickly confessing it and getting rid of it. We are exhorted in God's Word to be slow to anger and not to let the sun go down on our anger (James 1:19, Ephesians 4:26). But too often, this misunderstood "Nice Christian" way simply sweeps anger under the rug and never explores what's really going on inside the person.

One character in *Steel Magnolias* is a Christian named Annelle. She uses the Nice Christian approach when, seeing her husband put beer in the refrigerator, she pours it out and says, "I think we should pray . . . God, this makes me angry. I shouldn't be angry. I confess my sin and ask You to forgive me, and help me not to feel this way." Annelle assumes that anger is sinful in itself and must be acknowledged and taken to God to make it go away.

Obviously, it is right to acknowledge anger and certainly appropriate to pray about it, but before it is quickly dismissed through shallow self-condemnation and blanket confession, our anger needs to be explored. Often when we get below the surface reaction of anger, we see the deeper, more pervasive sin that needs repentance.

THE HONEST VOLCANO

A third style is to handle anger like an "Honest Volcano" with self-justification. The assumption here is that unexpressed or pent-up anger will cause problems, so it must be vocalized, released, and gotten out of one's system. Venting anger is justified and even glorified.

Ouisar, another character in *Steel Magnolias*, epitomizes this approach in every line she speaks. She glories in her anger, always has a bone to pick with somebody, and claims, "I'm not crazy! I've just been in a bad mood for forty years," and "Don't try to get on my good side; I don't have one!"

Today it is fashionable, like Ouisar, to dump our emotional baggage on others—whether through primal scream therapy or recovery groups that encourage members to forthrightly confront their mothers, fathers, or spouses with evidence of the damage they've done. But too often what happens in venting episodes is that, while there may be a temporary feeling of relief, all kinds of painful emotions are dislodged in both the Volcano and his or her target, and people are left to bleed internally. Once their deeper wounds have been exposed, Honest Volcanoes seem even more committed to greater anger as the only means of survival, the only way to cover up their agonizing aches. Eventually, this "Honest Volcano" approach protects no one and damages everyone, pushing people away and leaving oneself hardened and isolated.

2. a. Which of these three styles of handling anger (if any) is most like your style? Explain.

❑ Steel Magnolia

❑ Nice Christian

❑ Honest Volcano

b. If none of these three sounds like you, how would you describe your style?

3. Often our perceptions of ourselves differ from the way others see us. If you feel comfortable, ask those in your group to describe their views of how you deal with anger. Are there any differences?

LEADER: While reading the next section, the group members should think about what it would look like to use anger for the sake of love.

ANGER FOR LOVE

There is an alternative: using our anger for the sake of love. It involves not a series of steps, but rather a change of heart. While it is God's business to change us at this deepest level, we can certainly cultivate character traits and godly practices.

One is the Matthew 7 principle of examining ourselves first before "picking a bone" with someone else. In our sinful human nature we'd prefer to operate on another before submitting ourselves to soul surgery. Yet we have no right to presume to place our self-righteous anger on others when we have our own unexamined and well-protected reservoir of sin.

James 1:19-20 says, "Everyone should be quick to listen, slow to speak, and slow to become angry, for man's anger does not bring about the righteous life that God desires." This slowness to anger comes as God's Spirit produces patience, gentleness, and self-control in our lives. We need to commit ourselves by faith to love and seek others' welfare. How different we would be if Galatians 5:6 were our life theme: "The only thing that counts is faith expressing itself through love."

While we are examining our own lives, seeking to be slow to anger, and praying for the Lord to change our sinful and angry hearts, what are we to do when feelings of anger surge within us? We've seen what *not*

49

to do in the approaches of the Steel Magnolias, the Nice Christians, and the Honest Volcanoes.

We need to recognize our anger through its many disguises and think through its dynamics. What does it look like? What destructive symptoms need to be forsaken? Where is our rage coming from? Do the sources of our anger lie in our own selfish and demanding hearts? How are we using our anger sinfully to function for us and to protect ourselves?

Only after we've examined these dynamics should we decide whether or not to express our anger. The criteria here is not doing whatever feels good, nor avoiding whatever feels bad, but pursuing a commitment to love and minister to others. We need to be familiar with our own typical approach to handling our anger and beware of automatically falling into repeated patterns. Often those who tend to express their anger through confrontation need to consider simply praying about the situation. Those who tend to dismiss or avoid facing their anger may need to deal with it head on.

FOR, OR AGAINST?

Psalm 4:4 says, "In your anger do not sin; when you are on your beds, search your hearts and be silent." In searching our hearts, we need to ask ourselves these questions: Is the anger we are feeling *for* or *against* others? Is it profitable or harmful anger?

Anger *against* others is motivated by self-righteousness, pride, and greed. It is not concerned with the welfare of others, but is more interested in getting even and making others pay for their presumed offenses. Such anger contains no sorrow over another's sin, no compassion or forgiveness for sinners, and no recognition of one's own similar predicament (as a sinner in need of God's grace).

If locked inside, harmful anger takes the form of contempt and retreat: Melanie was so angry against her abuser that she desired to butcher him. She tried to lock those feelings deep inside her, but they snuck out

50

in destructive behavior against herself. But if openly expressed, anger *against* others desires to conquer and master them. Ouisar, the "Honest Volcano," lived to be "one up" on others by attacking them first, lest she be attacked. She used her anger to intimidate and control, and for the most part it worked.

Anger *for* the sake of others is quite different. While being centered on others, this profitable anger is motivated by love and energizes the self to move toward others for their good. Anger *for* others is costly, because it requires a broken heart that does not avoid pain but enters it and is changed.

A parent whose adult child steals the family's money and squanders it in illegal activities has the opportunity to use his or her anger for the sake of the son or daughter.

By pursuing the prodigal, firmly confronting him with his sin, and welcoming him home, the parent can choose to give the child a taste of the gospel. Perhaps they would work out a repayment plan over a number of years. But more important than repaying the debt would be reestablishing the relationship and committing themselves to deal with their own issues that contributed to the problem in the first place.

Each of us develops our own styles of handling anger. Our approach may be similar to the "Steel Magnolia," the "Nice Christian," or the "Honest Volcano," or it may be another style altogether. But chances are, our solutions to handling anger are not solutions at all without a change of heart wrought by the Holy Spirit. In the final session, we'll look at what it means to be healed from our anger so we can use this powerful emotion *for* instead of *against* others.

4. Give an example of how you have used your anger *against* others.

5. Have you ever used your anger *for* the sake of others? Give an example.

6. What seem to be the difficult parts of learning to use anger for love?

7. *(Optional)* Discuss the following biblical passages and their implications for handling anger.

   a. James 1:19-20. Why do you suppose being quick to listen and slow to speak helps in handling anger?

   b. Matthew 7:3-4. Think of a recent situation in which you've been angry. What was the "plank" in your eye? If you can't tell, describe the situation to the group and ask them what your blind spot might be.

   c. Philippians 2:4. What would be the other person's best interest in the case you named? For instance, would it be better to confront or to say nothing yet?

STILLNESS

Talk with God about the difficulties you noted in question 6. Each person should have a chance to ask God for one thing regarding learning to use anger for love.

> LEADER: In your final session, you may want to look again at the list of questions about anger the members raised at the beginning of session 1. Remember to bring that list to your next meeting.

DURING THE WEEK

When you're angry this week, try to identify your anger's *symptoms*, its *sources*, and the *functions* it achieves for you. Look also at your overall *style* of handling anger. Fill out the following chart for at least one angry episode.

SYMPTOMS OF MY ANGER

I express by:

I repress by:

Sources of my anger (my goals that were blocked):

Functions it achieves for me (see list on page 43):

Styles of handling my anger:

HEALING FROM ANGER

ই৯

1. As you've tried to identify the symptoms, sources, functions, and style of your anger, what would you say is one thing that continues to perplex you about your anger? What is one difficulty you are having?

> LEADER: Give everyone a chance to respond to question 1. Then ask participants to look for an answer to what perplexes them as this material is read aloud.

Okay, we understand we're infected with anger that has destructive symptoms and ungodly goals and functions. How can we pursue healing from this anger disease?

GOD'S ANGER

The human portraits of anger we've looked at stand in sharp contrast to the righteous anger of God. The Old Testament is filled with passionate descriptions of His "burning anger." The song of praise in Exodus 15 recounts God's display of anger in the Red Sea thrashing. The graphic language in verses 7 and 8 paints a terrifying picture of sinners in the hands of an angry God: "You unleashed your burning anger; it consumed them like stubble. By the blast of your nostrils the waters piled up. The surging waters stood firm like a wall; the deep waters congealed in the heart of the sea."

Again in Exodus 22, the Lord declares the potential power of His anger to the Israelites in the following command: "Do not take advantage of a widow or an orphan. If you do, . . . my anger will be aroused and I will kill you" (verses 22-24). Then, in response to the golden calf incident, God is enraged and tells Moses, "Leave me alone so that my anger may burn against them [the stiff-necked people]" (32:10).

Jesus, too, was often angry. In Matthew 4:10 Jesus angrily orders Satan away from Him and fights for God's glory: "For it is written: 'Worship the Lord your God, and serve him only.'" He also demonstrates His zeal for His Father's honor when at the beginning of His ministry (John 2) and again toward the end of His earthly life (Matthew 21), He vents His anger at the moneychangers in the temple, overturning their tables and driving them out.

When Jesus had the opportunity to heal a man's withered hand on the Sabbath, He "looked around at them [the Pharisees] in anger" (Mark 3:5) because they were waiting for a reason to accuse Him and to justify plotting His death. Jesus was not only angry at the Pharisees, but also "deeply distressed at their stubborn hearts," yet He did not let that prevent His work of love and healing in restoring the man's hand.

Even with His own disciples, Jesus was often upset at their selfishness and ignorance. In Mark 10:13-15, He is indignant at the disciples for rebuking those who were bringing little children to Him. In Matthew 16:23, as we have already seen, Jesus rebukes Peter for opposing His claim that He must suffer and be killed.

WHAT IS RIGHTEOUS ANGER?

What does God's anger show us about righteous anger? First of all, righteous anger is *not self-protective*, but is extended for the good of the other. In the examples above, God acted to protect the Israelites at the Red Sea, for the sake of widows and orphans, and to stamp out idolatry and foster loyalty and holiness in His people. Jesus' anger was propelled by His love for the Father and His commitment to serve only Him, by His zeal for righteousness in the temple, by His hatred of hypocrisy and legalism, by His desire to heal and touch others, and finally by His willingness to sacrifice His life for His sheep.

Righteous anger is *motivated from a pure heart* that *focuses on the things of God*, rather than the things of self and men. Righteous anger is *aroused by a hatred of sin* and sustained by *sacrificial giving* for the sake of others.

As often as the Bible reveals divine anger, the most frequently repeated reference to God's anger is, "The LORD is compassionate and gracious, *slow to anger*, abounding in love" (Psalm 103:8, emphasis added; see also Exodus 34:6, Numbers 14:18, Nehemiah 9:17, Psalm 86:15, Joel 2:13, Jonah 4:2, Nahum 1:3). Righteous anger is not only patient, restrained, and controlled, but it is also coupled with love and grace. Righteous anger is like godly discipline, which Hebrews 12 describes as a sure sign of the Father's deep love for His children. It is energy expended on behalf of loved ones.

Unfortunately, our anger falls far short of the righteous anger of the Lord. How can we change so that we don't use anger to cover our wounds and launch a counterattack against others? *We need to allow our anger to sink us deeper into the underlying reality of our own sadness and sorrow: the sadness of living in a fallen world and a sorrow over sin.*

SADNESS AND SORROW

If anger is unpleasant, how much more are sadness and sorrow, since we use the former to avoid the latter!

Perhaps some of us easily understand why we want to escape weeping over the damage our sin has caused or why we try to elude the pain of our own wounds.

Neither pain nor sin can be deeply grieved without God. We spend our lives trying to grow in independence, build our resources, and strengthen our capacity to handle whatever comes our way. Why, then, would we ever choose to admit we can't function independently because our need is greater than we can fill? We choose anger to blind or shield us from the deeper reality of this fallen world and our sinful selves because we can't fix or manage them on our own. The self-protective reaction of anger allows us to carry around hidden hurts and needs rather than take them to the only One who can ultimately shoulder them and offer healing: God the Father.

Anger that is not primarily for the sake of others and is not honestly, controllably, and sacrificially dealt with *in sorrow* is tainted with sin. Our anger will never be 100 percent pure like the Lord's, but we can grow by sincerely confessing our self-centered anger. As we have seen, it is often rooted in the selfishness of not getting what we want, and it usually functions as sinful self-protection, revealing our own demandingness, arrogance, and lack of faith in a sovereign and loving God.

Instead of denying our anger or lashing out with it, we need to recognize it as a *signal of something much deeper going on inside us.* Anger will blind us to our own wrongdoing if we don't look deeper than our anger to see the root of our sin and experience our own need for God's merciful forgiveness. We need to hush our anger and be silenced by the sin of our selfishness that runs throughout our hearts. Only then will the gospel of Jesus' free payment for our sins and His all-forgiving love become good news to us. We need to be so captured by grace that our love for and gratitude to God far outshine the fire of our anger.

How will we ever be healed from our anger? Only by seeing how much we deserve God's wrath, but instead have been graciously spared from the eternal consequences of rebellion against Him through faith in Christ.

2. Look at Psalm 18:1-19. You don't have to read the whole passage aloud, but notice the anger God displays (verses 7-15) and the reason He displays it (verses 6,16-19). How easy is it for you to believe deeply that God might be angry *on your behalf, for your good*? Explain.

3. a. Think of someone with whom you're angry. What hurt might lie behind that anger? It could be hurt from that person recently, or from someone in your past.

   b. How do you feel when you think about that hurt? (Sad? Numb? Angry? Confused?)

4. a. What damage has your sinful anger done to others? Give some examples.

   b. How do you feel when you think about that?

5. How has your perspective on anger changed during the course of this study?

6. In what new ways do you expect you'll be handling your anger?

7. Look back at the list of questions about anger you raised in session 1. Which have been answered? Which haven't? What would you like to do about that?

STILLNESS

Spend some time thanking God for what you've learned from these discussions about anger. You can ask God to answer questions you still have about anger. You can also ask Him to continue showing you what's going on inside you that lies behind your anger.

DURING THE WEEK

Set aside some time to think about (1) the hurt behind your anger and (2) ways you've damaged others by your anger.

HELP FOR LEADERS

✍

This guide is designed to be discussed in a group of from four to twelve people. Because God has designed Christians to function as a body, we learn and grow more when we interact with others than we would on our own. If you are on your own, see if you can recruit a few other people to join you in working through this guide. You can use the guide on your own, but you'll probably long for someone to talk with about it. On the other hand, if you have a group larger than twelve we suggest that you divide into smaller groups of six or so for discussion. With more than twelve people, you begin to move into a large group dynamic, and not everyone has the opportunity to participate.

The following pages are designed to help a discussion leader guide the group in an edifying time centered on God's truth and grace. You may want one appointed person to lead all the sessions, or you may want to rotate leadership.

PREPARATION

Your aim as a leader is to create an environment that encourages people to feel safe enough to be honest with themselves, the group, and God. Group members should sense that no question is too dumb to ask, that

61

the other participants will care about them no matter what they reveal about themselves, and that each person's opinion is as valid as everyone else's. At the same time, they should know that the Bible is your final authority for what is true.

As the group leader, your most important preparation for each session is prayer. You will want to make your prayers personal, of course, but here are some suggestions:

- Pray that group members will be able to attend the discussion consistently. Ask God to enable them to feel safe enough to share vulnerable thoughts and feelings honestly, and to contribute their unique gifts and insights.

- Pray for group members' private times with God. Ask Him to be active in nurturing each person.

- Ask the Holy Spirit for guidance in exercising patience, acceptance, sensitivity, and wisdom. Pray for an atmosphere of genuine love in the group, with each member being honestly open to learning and change.

- Pray that your discussion will lead each of you to obey the Lord more closely and demonstrate His presence to others.

- Pray for insight and wisdom as you lead the group.

After prayer, your most important preparation is to be thoroughly familiar with the material you will discuss. Before each meeting, be sure to read the text and answer all of the questions for yourself. This will prepare you to think ahead of questions group members might raise.

Choose a time and place to meet that is consistent, comfortable, and relatively free from distractions. Refreshments can help people mingle, but don't let this consume your study and discussion time.

LEADING THE GROUP

It should be possible to cover each session in sixty minutes, but you will probably find yourself wishing you had two hours to talk about each group member's situation. As you conduct each session keep the following in mind.

Work toward a safe, relaxed, and open atmosphere. This may not come quickly, so as the leader you must model acceptance, humility, openness to truth and change, and love. Develop a genuine interest in each person's remarks, and expect to learn from them. Show that you care by listening carefully. Be affirming and sincere. Sometimes a hug is the best response—sometimes a warm silence is.

Pay attention to how you ask questions. By your tone of voice, convey your interest in and enthusiasm for the question and your warmth toward the group. The group members will adopt your attitude. Read the questions as though you were asking them of good friends.

If the discussion falters, keep these suggestions in mind:

- Be comfortable with silence. Let the group wrestle to think of answers. Some of the questions require thought or reflection on one's life. Don't be quick to jump in and rescue the group with your answers.

- On the other hand, you should answer questions yourself occasionally. In particular, you should be the first to answer questions about personal experiences. In this way you will model the depth of vulnerability you hope others will show. Count on this: If you are open, others will be too, and vice versa. Don't answer every question, but don't be a silent observer.

- Reword a question if you perceive that the group has trouble understanding it as written.

- If a question evokes little response, feel free to leave it and move on.

- When discussion is winding down on a question, go on to the next one. It's not necessary to push people to see every angle.

Ask only one question at a time. Often, participants' responses will suggest a follow-up question to you. Be discerning as to when you are following a fruitful train of thought and when you are going on a tangent.

Be aware of time. It's important to honor the commitment to end at a set time.

Encourage constructive controversy. The group members can learn a great deal from struggling with the many sides of an issue. If you aren't threatened when someone disagrees, the whole group will be more open and vulnerable. Intervene when necessary, making sure that people debate ideas and interpretations, not attack each other's feelings or character. If the group gets stuck in an irreconcilable argument, say something like, "We can agree to disagree here," and move on.

Be someone who facilitates, rather than an expert. People feel more prone to contribute with a peer leader than with a "parent" leader. Allow the group members to express their feelings and experiences candidly.

Encourage autonomy with the group members. With a beginning group, you may have to ask all the questions and do all the planning. But within a few meetings you should start delegating various leadership tasks. Help members learn to exercise their gifts. Let them start making decisions and solving problems together. Encourage them to maturity and unity in Christ.

Validate both feelings and objective facts. Underneath the umbrella of Scripture, there is room for both. Often, people's feelings are a road map to a biblical truth. Give them permission for feelings and facts.

Summarize the discussion. Summarizing what has been said will help the group members see where the discussion is going and keep them more focused.

Don't feel compelled to "finish." It would be easy to spend an entire session on one or two questions. As leader, you will be responsible to decide when to cut off one discussion and move to another question, and when to let a discussion go on even though you won't have time for some questions. If there are more questions than you need, you can select those that seem most helpful.

Let the group plan applications. The "During the Week" sections are suggestions. Your group should adapt them to be relevant and life-changing for the members. If people see a genuine need that an application addresses, they are more likely to follow up. Help them see the connection between need and application.

End with refreshments. This gives people an excuse to stay for a few extra minutes and discuss the subject informally. Often the most important conversations occur after the formal session.

DURING THE FIRST SESSION

You or someone else in the group can open the session with a short prayer dedicating your time to God.

It is significant how much more productive and honest a discussion is if the participants know each other. The questions in this session are designed to help participants get acquainted. You can set an example of appropriate disclosure by being the first to answer some questions. Participants will be looking to you to let them know how much honesty is safe in this group. If you reveal your worst secrets in the first session, you may scare some people away. Conversely, if you conceal anything that might make you look bad, participants will get the message that honesty isn't safe.

Prior to launching into the discussion, go over the following guidelines. They will help make your discussion more fruitful, especially when you're dealing with issues that truly matter to people.

Confidentiality. No one should repeat what someone shares in the group unless that person gives permission. Even then, discretion is imperative. Be trustworthy. Participants should talk about their own feelings and experiences, not those of others.

Attendance. Each session builds on previous ones, and you need continuity with each other. Ask group members to commit to attending all six sessions unless an emergency arises.

Participation. This is a *group* discussion, not a lecture. It is important that each person participates in the group.

Honesty. Appropriate openness is a key to a good group. Be who you really are, not who you think you should be. On the other hand, don't reveal inappropriate details of your life simply for the shock value. The goal is relationship.

Following are some perspectives on a few questions from the sessions, in case your group finds any of them difficult to answer. These are not necessarily the "right" answers, but they should provide food for thought.

SESSION ONE

The purpose of this first session is to help participants identify what they already believe, deep down, about anger. Few of us have ever put those beliefs into words, but they lie behind the ways we habitually deal with our own and others' anger. It would be a good idea for each participant to write down a few of his or her beliefs about anger so that you can all keep those beliefs at the forefront of your minds as you move through the study.

SESSION TWO

Question 3. This is a hard but crucial question. It may not be immediately obvious why one person chooses to withdraw and overeat, while another yells and another makes jokes. Have each person look back at his or her answers to the questions in session 1, and see if those offer any clues. For example, the belief that "anger should be avoided at all costs" might be expected to lead to repressing anger, while "anger is a great way to get what I want" might more naturally lead to expressing it dramatically. If a man saw his mother use anger manipulatively to dominate his father, he might react by committing himself to holding the upper hand in angry confrontations. Some of us imitate our parents' behavior, while others react against it.

Question 5. Sometimes we choose as a target someone who is safer than others at whom we may be angry. For instance, a man may know that losing his temper at his boss or his mother will be disastrous, while blowing up at his wife or his children will cause him much less pain. A woman may detest her mother in order to preserve her fantasy that her father has always loved and cared for her. Many of us decide that the safest person at whom to vent our anger is ourselves.

At other times we may choose someone who is the epitome of the person(s) we're angry at. We may resent all authority figures, but a supervisor may become our focus. A husband may represent all the abusive men in a woman's life.

SESSION FOUR

Question 3. Inflicting pain on someone else is obviously unloving. By snuffing out our tenderness we spurn God's efforts to replace our heart of stone with one of flesh (Ezekiel 11:19, 36:26). Hiding our own sin enables us to persist in it. Some people may find it hard to see how soothing their own pain is wrong, so you may need to talk about this in more depth. Hiding our pain is wrong because it's an effort to make our lives work without God. We'd rather do anything than have to go to God, broken and desperate.

Question 4. Righteous anger genuinely has the other person's best at heart. You'll explore this more in session 5.